Having grown up in North Wales, spent five years in London, and now currently living in Oxfordshire with her husband, Jonathan, and sons, Harry and Gabriel, Rosie has written poetry for as long as she can remember. A self-professed 'hoarder of words', she still has copies of her very first poems about bunny rabbits and the sun, and every poem she has written since, as she grew and used her writing to make sense of the world around her and to navigate life's trials and tribulations. Rosie has always found connection in the raw and relatable words of other writers and hopes to be able to provide the same to readers with her poetry.

For Olivia – our love for you is endless. Thank you for everything you brought to us, for showing us how grief and love can live side by side.

Rosie Phillips

IF I COULD WRITE YOU INTO LIFE

AUSTIN MACAULEY PUBLISHERS™

LONDON · CAMBRIDGE · NEW YORK · SHARJAH

Copyright © Rosie Phillips 2024

The right of Rosie Phillips to be identified as author of this work has been asserted by the author in accordance with sections 77 and 78 of the Copyright, Designs and Patents Act 1988.

All rights reserved. No part of this publication may be reproduced, stored in a retrieval system, or transmitted in any form or by any means, electronic, mechanical, photocopying, recording, or otherwise, without the prior permission of the publishers.

Any person who commits any unauthorised act in relation to this publication may be liable to criminal prosecution and civil claims for damages.

A CIP catalogue record for this title is available from the British Library.

ISBN 9781035828852 (Paperback)
ISBN 9781035828869 (ePub e-book)

www.austinmacauley.co.uk

First Published 2024
Austin Macauley Publishers Ltd®
1 Canada Square
Canary Wharf
London
E14 5AA

Jonathan – thank you for always being my biggest fan and for never tiring of listening to my words. I love you.

Rosie and Luke – thank you for trusting me to write about Archie, I feel honoured to have known and loved him for his two years here. I will carry him with me for life.

There is a well-versed saying that grief is just love with no place to go. Perhaps it is not just a saying at all; it very well could be fact. A definite fact of grief is that it is universal. Grief will touch us all at one point or another, in one way or another, and we will search desperately for ways to cope, for connection; for grief is ever so lonely. I try to navigate grief through writing. And so, through the losses in my life, particularly the loss of our baby through missed-miscarriage, *If I Could Write You Into Life* was born. The irony of the birth of a book in the wake of a loss of baby is not lost on me. My only hope for this book is that maybe, if you're reading this in the depths of sorrow, if you too are missing a bump to stroke or a tiny hand to hold, that you feel a little less alone. I know I cannot take away your pain, but I hope that through these pages I can sit with you in it, and hold your hand.

Filing

In the moments that followed
and the days that dragged,
I took all the dreams I had
that were once plans for you and me,
and I filed them under memories
of everything that could have been.

You Belong with Me

I find comfort in your comfort;
lay in the home I made for you.
Even with no air to breathe,
no strength in your heart to pump again,
you nestled tighter in my womb.
You told me, "I belong with you."

And there you remained,
peaceful in the silence,
comfortable in the stillness
of the only home you had ever known.

I am sorry that you have to go.
I promise, it won't hurt.
I'll lay you gently in the earth.

And I have made you a new home,
the forever kind,
in the warmth of my heart
and the embrace of my mind.

Waiting

You wait to try.
You wait for two lines.
You wait for nine months.
Your baby, the prize.

Pregnancy is a test in patience,
practice, they say, for parenting;
for the long nights and hard days,
for the thousand songs you tire to sing.

Here I am, I am waiting.
No one tells you this – surprise!
No one tells you about the waiting
when the love you're growing dies.

Waiting in seats, waiting rooms,
for your turn on the bed;
waiting to be suffocated
with the news your baby's dead.

Waiting for answers, waiting for reasons,
they never seem to come.
Waiting for the 'next steps' talk;
the next step no longer 'Mum.'

And now, I'm here, I'm waiting,
foetal in my bed
to welcome you to join us;
to welcome home the dead.

I am waiting for you here.
I can feel you're on your way,
passing silently from mother to Earth,
from womb's water to the clay.

Irony

The aching irony of the postnatal pads,
thick like mattresses between my thighs.
The plastic-backed sheet I have known before,
recovery ward buddies of old.
Now a visitor in my home.

No, the irony is not lost on me,
the way that your body is lost to me.

I Love You Just as Much

When I saw you lay so still upon the screen,
I thought that I might never get to hold you in my hands.
Yet here you are,
still as ever,
sat in my hands,
my perfect baby.

How I wish you could have grown
to fit within my arms.
Yet still, I love you just as much,
a few centimetres in my palm.

Enough

Your eyes were black like coal,
but I guess you never saw.
Your brain swollen with a mind,
never given chance for thoughts.
Your hands were stretched out,
longing for a touch,
and so I cradled you in my palm
and I prayed it was enough.

Tonight

The moon is small tonight;
fragile, smooth silhouette,
yet it shines so bright.

It modelled itself on you
as you flew
to light up the eternal night.

The Sun Was Too Bright

The sun was too bright
through my window
on the Friday that I waited for you.

I lay on my bed,
eyes squinting at the light
and I cried as I waited for you.

And when my tears dried,
my mind, it focused;
I knew there was not long left to wait for you.

And in the bright of the sun,
in the heat of the day,
from the warmth of my womb you came away.

I was no longer waiting for you.

But the sun was too bright
through my window that day
that you came to me.

Because with your leaving
came the blackest of nights.
It will last for eternity.

I Found You

The next day I found you again,
though you already lay in the earth.

When the pain floored me,
cool release of tiles on longing skin,
my eyes caught sight of you once more;
just one splash of crimson
low down on the bathroom door.

I sat with you a while.
The only physical remnants of your life
lying this side of the garden soil.
I stared, I breathed, I wiped the blood away.

And there my womb cried out
to hold you just one more day.

Your Daddy

Your daddy, he writes songs for you.
He writes the words he does not say.
He sings for you in the evening light,
and he thinks of you all day.

Your daddy, he writes songs for you.
As he plays them, tears fall.
He sings songs for you in the moonlight,
and through the earth you hear them all.

Your daddy, he writes songs for you.
He writes them through the night.
His songs are filled with the love he'd give,
if he could only hold you tight.

Your daddy, he writes songs for you.
He sings them through his pain.
As he sings, and his heart lays bare,
through his voice you live again.

What I Wouldn't Give

What I wouldn't give
not to have run out of vases.
Not to have two windowsills
filled with the most beautiful flowers,
busy with cards,
bursting with love,
with kind words and well wishes.

What I wouldn't give
to have no phone calls,
no messages of love,
not to hear people say over and over again
that they have no words.

What I wouldn't give
for my friends to have words for me:
Words like "congratulations,"
"great news!"
"I can't wait to meet her."
"She looks just like you."

But they have no words.
There are no words.
And I am grateful for their love;
for the gifts,
for the cards,
for the windowsills full of flowers
that fill my home with sweet scent and well wishes.
I promise, I am grateful.

But what I wouldn't give
for bare sills,
for no post,
for a flower-less home,
an empty inbox,
an unbroken heart beating in my chest
and another in my womb.

Blossom Baby

You're now my blossom baby,
the month of March belongs to you,
and with each spring, the trees will save me,
with each gentle leaf, a breath of you.

Delicate in the warming air,
they flutter as I pass;
and in the sweetness of their scent,
your memory forever lasts.

Goodbye, my blossom baby.
We must leave your body in the spring,
but your love will travel seasons
with the bitter sadness that does bring.

Goodbye, my blossom baby,
beneath the sticky, dewy, ground.
Though we lost you in the springtime,
in our hearts you're always found.

A last goodbye, my blossom baby,
more beautiful than the trees;
I stroked your petal skin
as you departed on the breeze.

Forever Spring

You were supposed to be autumn to me;
earthy hues,
crunchy leaves,
evolving colours beneath our feet.

But you became forever spring;
pastel flowers,
birds that sing,
new life and the irony that it brings.

I will see you in every blossom,
feel you in the morning dew.
With your passing, now and always,
the spring belongs to you.

Stars

I wish upon the stars
and they shine their fire through the night.

In their sparkle, I see your eyes.
In their glow, I feel your life.

But just like you they sink
in the darkness forevermore.
I can never hold them tight,
though they are with me I am sure.

In Bloom

Did you know the whole world is in bloom?
Bursting with love, swollen with pride.
There is a growing shadow around every corner,
one for every tear that I've cried.

I don't want the world to stop blooming;
I would hate to watch it wilt.
I just want to plant a flower here
and not be laden down with guilt.

I want to bloom here with the world;
there's a bud on every tree.
But bark still cracks and sap seeps out;
that sap belonged to me.

I do know the whole world is in bloom,
but its beauty is bitter-sweet.
It's hard to see birds singing
when you cannot hear a single tweet.

Life Counted in Weeks

"How many weeks?"
that is what I keep being asked.
"How far along?"
"Was it early?"

As if the number of times
your cells multiplied
should somehow make it easier
for me to cope with the fact that you died.

"At least it was now, not later."
Like I should be grateful
to have bled a life,
when I could have birthed
a full-grown baby that died.
As though that was the only other option.

What about the third option?
Me holding my child,
watching her grow older,
ride bikes, fall down, run wild;

but no, not for them.
They just want to tell me that
I should be grateful
that sanitary towels
could catch my future
as she fell between my thighs.

Mother's Day

Really, it's for all of you.
The Hallmark cards will have you believe
you need to fit a certain mould:
Birth mother, visible mother,
happy, smiling, arms full mother.

But today is for all of you.
It is for all of us.

For the mothers with arms full,
for the mothers with arms empty,
For the mothers with arms half full.
For the mothers who see their babies in the stars,
in photo albums and memories,
but never on their knee.
For the mothers who had to give their babies back,
for the expectant mothers,
for the cautiously hopeful mothers,
for the adoptive and the foster mothers.

Today belongs to all of you.
Today is all of ours.

The Hallmark message might not fit
the hand that you have been dealt;
the motherhood that's so damn hard.
But this day is for you,
with, or without, a card.

Two Trees

Two trees, they grew together
planted side by side.
They were watered just the same,
neither was denied.

They made their roots deep below,
amongst the safest earth.
Pushing towards the surface,
ready for their birth.

The two trees drew a map
of life below the ground,
preparing for the day
they would make their earthly sound.

The two trees they grew together
planted side by side,
but as one burst through to meet the sun,
the other tree had died.

One tree is growing above the earth,
standing tall and green.
The bones of the other tree
are withering, unseen.

Two trees are planted in the earth,
their homes lay side by side,
both as precious as the other;
even though our tree has died.

Just the Three of Us

It was a March day like no other
that has been nor will hopefully come again.
The first one contained,
restrained by the invisible illness
for which, that day, I did not care about at all.

The feeling had been sitting with me for two weeks:
the fear,
the background noise,
the unwelcome voice,
that told me, "There's something wrong."

But I squashed it.
I crushed it.
I pushed it down and boxed it.
Told it that it was unwelcome here:
a liar,
a liar.
It had to be a liar.

And yet on this day the truth spilled free,
projected on the screen.
Utter silence.
Completely still.
The heart I saw flicker with life once,
now invisible amongst the greyscale;
a canvas for death.

Tears ran and sobs echoed.
Alone.
Alone.
More alone than I had ever known.

Just us three:
A doctor, my dead baby, and me.

In My Subconscious You Live On

I'm not sleeping at night
when you're floating through my mind,
dominating the darkness.

And when I am finally exhausted by you,
when my body aches from thoughts
of you and who you could be,
my weary eyes, they close at last
and still I am graced no peace.

Because there you sit, clearer still;
the master of my subconscious,
ready to show me how you feel,
who you are and all you will ever be,
trapped within the confines of my skull
and never my arms.

The Waves That Break You

The words build and crest into a wave,
they wash away in one fell swoop
those who would rather not know;
resigning those that you considered friends
to far off shores where they cannot hear your pain.

Left wading through the crashing tide
are the forever friends.
Already knee deep in your cries
they keep on paddling.
They are the ones who hold you in your grief,
with no real understanding of it;
just life-floats built from love and the hope
that they can somehow help.

When you stand as tall as shaking knees allow
and say aloud, "My baby died,"
the tide rushes out,
closing doors on its way.

Then it washes slowly in and with it, new faces,
dragged against their will;
new bodies, semi-drowned in their own grief,
wide eyed, one hand raised in the air,
the other helplessly thrashing to change the tide.

And now the shore upon which you stand
is a little less lonely.
They stumble to their feet,
spit out the water they were sure would kill them
and they say, "Mine too."
"My baby died too."

The Fog

Have you not noticed the fog?
You are talking to me through it
as though it's not all around,
as though it doesn't fill the earth
from the sky to the ground.

Have you not noticed the fog?
You are walking with me through it
as though you find it so easy,
as though it doesn't infiltrate your lungs.
You can't hear me wheezing.

Have you not noticed the fog?
You are acting like you haven't seen it,
as though you don't understand.
It's so heavy, it's so dense
that I can barely stand.

I need you to notice the fog,
even if you cannot see it,

I need you to notice me plead.
This fog, it's choking,
it's suffocating me.

The Brightest Stars

It is often said, "They're the brightest stars
lighting up the night."

I feel they're the breath of the air,
the gentle breeze that lifts the hair
upon your skin
and makes you feel, momentarily,
more alive than you have
since the moment they left.

They come to remind you
that you live on;
and for as long as you do,
they will too.

You Are Not Today

Today is your day,
but you are not today.

To me you will always be the moon,
when it shines so bright, so sharp,
as the night you left.

To me you will always be the memories
that I hold of you, of holding you,
so small – there's so few.

To me you will be every day since you left
and every day yet to come when I think of you
and who you might have been.

To me you will be every time I look lovingly
at your siblings, and wonder would you look like them
if only you had stayed.

To me you will be every tear that has fallen
in your wake, finding its way into words
on pages such as this one.

To me you will always be the ache
in the hollow of my chest, when I'm breathless
from the thought of you.

To me you will always be the photos I cherish,
the memory of you growing within,
the stretching of my skin.

To me you will always be your birthday,
every year; the day I held you in my hands
for the first and last time.

But you are not today.

Though we honour you, though we take time,
though my heart hangs heavy,
you are not today.

You are not your due date.
For you are no longer due.

The Club

Welcome to the club.
There will be no welcome tea,
no biscuits or crust-less sandwiches
on a platter, sitting pretty.

Welcome to the club.
It's like none you've ever known;
no name badges, no meet and greet.
You'll enter it alone.

But you are not alone.

Welcome to the club.
You will be forced in through the door.
And when you turn around to leave,
the handle is no more.

Welcome to the club.
You're a member from now on.
No cancel button, no unsubscribe,
they haven't got it wrong.

If you faced your fellow members,
you'd see they're just like you,
searching for the exit sign,
wishing it weren't true.

Welcome to the club,
tear-stained faces and vacant eyes.
This club of missing babies
where hope comes to die.

I Remember You

And though you were so little, frail in the palm of my hand,
what you gave to us was bigger than we ever could have
planned.

I remember you as a positive test, as two blue lines,
as a joyous text.
I remember you as a giddy phone call, or three.
I remember you as our first scan, a nervous hand
and happy tears.
I remember you as a little heart beating, on the screen
and inside me.

I remember you as the moment I told your brother you were
ours;
as a happy hug, an excited jump.
I remember you as my growing bump, as our future hope
in tightening clothes.
I remember you because I am your mother, no matter what,
I always will be.

I remember you laid so still in the palm of my hand, skin like paper,
eyes like coal.
I remember you so, so small.
I remember you as the few hours we spent together, same side of the womb,
same side of the earth.

I remember you as words I spoke to ears that could not hear.
I remember you and hope that somehow you could;
that somehow you knew I was holding you tight,
that it did not hurt to take flight.
I remember you and hope that, somehow, you were alright.

But mostly, I remember you as the gift you gave us.
I remember you not only as your one life, but as two,
intersected and intertwined.
I remember you leaving the door open on your way out,
to let your little brother in, to help heal our hearts.

I remember you, and I always will.

Pictures

My baby sits in pictures,
yours sits within the pram.
You're busy making memories,
whilst I cling to those I can.

My baby's slowly fading,
friends no longer say her name.
They look upon your babe with love,
mine forgotten with my pain.

I cannot see the difference.
I do not understand why
my baby must be forgotten
just because she had to die.

So my baby sits in pictures,
I place them everywhere.
She cannot be forgotten
when she is clearly there.

And yet, somehow, they manage
to act as though she's not.
They turn their eyes away
as though they have forgot

all those times they told me,
in the days after she died,
she would never be forgotten,
as they wiped the tears I cried.

They held my hands in theirs,
they asked me for her name.
They treated me as though
my baby was the same.

All it took was a little time,
to undo the words they said.
Because my baby sits in pictures,
but my baby she is dead.

My baby sits in pictures
that they do not wish to feel.
So I place the pictures everywhere,
to remind them she is real.

Let Me Tell You (On This, My Third Mother's Day Here)

If you look for your baby in rainbows,
in robins or the stars.
If your windowsill is bursting
or you're missing little cards,
if your arms are filled with heartbeats,
or the emptiness between;
this day belongs to you.
Let me tell you, you are seen.

If your house is filled with laughter
and the pattering of feet,
or a suffocating silence
that you just can't defeat,
if you spent this morning with a child,
when there should be two or more;
this day still belongs to you.
Let me tell you, I am sure.

If your baby lives in photographs,
sat upon the side,
or in your deepest wishes,

in the fear that you can't hide.
If your child now lives in memories,
no longer within your hands;
this day still belongs to you,
and when it's hard, I understand.

Breathe it in and breathe it out.
This day will soon pass by.
If you want to, then you can savour it,
but it's also fine to cry.
Make what you want of it,
but no matter what, be filled with pride,
for today belongs to all of you,
with children here and those who died.

The Rain Will Fall Less Often

The rain will fall less often,
but you'll always know it's there,
threatening to wipe you out
in one heavy shower,
to drown you once again.

And when it comes, it pours,
just like the first time.
It leaves you numb with the kind of cold
that infiltrates your bones
until you cannot get warm again.

But I promise, the only thing that I know,
hold on and the rain will fall less often.

I Sit Where You Lay, Dear Archie

We sit where you lay for a third season now.
None of us are yet sure just how.

Summer stole you like it steals the humidity from the air we breathe,
and so we began to sit where you lay.
We told stories to the dry earth, the thirsty birds, to the scolding sun.
We sang songs without water more than that which runs down cheeks,
and we began to sit where you lay.

The weeks moved forward ungraciously,
like they didn't know they were asked to stop.
Time itself did not do you the honour of taking the time to sit.
But yet, we came to sit where you lay.
Short sleeves to long, always our favourite song,
repeated books through blurry eyes under the sooner darkening skies.
Another season landed, we wrapped up and chose to sit where you lay.

And now in the third act, it has turned bitter;
rosy cheeks, numbed hands, the crunch of sugared grass as we sit where you lay.
On paper it should keep us away.
And yet, I find myself wanting to be with you even more, I cannot stay away.
I sit.
I sit.
I sit where you lay.

And though the reddening of my hands may burn, cheeks sting,
I know with no blood pumping, you must be colder.
And it consumes my thoughts,
my heart it breaks;
in my mind, I see you cold.

And so I come to you.
I pass you my love and warmth through the earth
as I sit where you lay.

The Birds

One day, you will breathe again.

The sound of birds will hit your inner ear
and you might even smile, no nausea
at the audacity of the world to keep on spinning,
the sun to keep on shining, those damn birds
to keep on singing. You might smile.

And you will breathe again.

You Are with Me, I Am Sure

For Archie, forever loved, forever missed, forever two.

If I close my eyes and hold them shut
just tight enough that the tears stay put
for a moment or two,
I can feel you.

If I can hold back the sobs in the depth of my chest
where they can no longer leave me gasping for breath,
for a moment or two,
I'm holding you.

In silent moments, in the times I'm alone,
if I can block the pain of your passing that cuts to the bone,
for a moment I'm sure
you're here once more.

I can remember the weight of your little body
leaning on mine.
I can hear you babble so gently in my ears.
Eyes closed, heart open; you're here.

You are sat upon my lap, and I read you a story.
You're showing me toys, you're holding my hand.
I can almost smell you; I promise I can.
In the silent dark, you're here in my arms.

If I can just hold this moment, lock it in time,
then you will live on forever, embraced by my mind.